Book 2
On Target

K. Agar and P. W. R. Foot

Illustrated by Sumiko Davis

M
Macmillan Education

First published 1977
Reprinted 1979, 1980

Macmillan Education Ltd
Houndmills, Basingstoke, Hampshire RG21 2XS
and London
Associated companies in New York, Dublin,
Melbourne, Johannesburg and Delhi

Printed in Hong Kong by
L. Rex Printing Co., Ltd.

Acknowledgements

The editors and publishers wish to thank the following who have kindly given permission for the
use of copyright material:

Faber & Faber Ltd for an extract from 'Night Mail' from *Collected Shorter Poems* by W. H. Auden;
David Higham Associates Ltd for an extract from 'Boy's and Girl's Names' from *Silver Sand and
Snow* by Eleanor Frajeon, published by Michael Joseph Ltd; Niall Macaulay for an extract from
'Wishes'; Methuen Children's Books Ltd and Charles Scriber's & Sons, for an extract from *The
Wind in the Willows* by Kenneth Grahame, reprinted by permission of the publishers and Text
Copyright University Chest Oxford; The Society of Authors and the Literary Trustees of Walter
de la Mare for an extract from 'The Shadow' by Walter de la Mare; Mrs A. M. Walsh for 'Under
the Pier' from *The Roundabout by the Sea* by John Walsh.

Contents

1 Games

Starting Points

Which games do you enjoy most—team games, or those you play with one or two friends?

What games depend on the weather?

Why are team games more popular with men than with women?

What team games are played by women?

What indoor games do you enjoy?

Would you rather play indoor games with grown-ups or with people of your own age?

Describe a game that you enjoy playing with adults.

Do we spend too much time *watching* games?

Words to Use

Look up the following words in a dictionary, and then use one of them to complete each of the sentences below.

*opponent   pavilion   referee   sport
score   tackle   umpire   commentary*

The ∗∗∗ blew his whistle, and the centre-forward kicked off.
The boxer punched his ∗∗∗ on the chin.
The half-back ran to ∗∗∗ the other team's centre-forward.
The ∗∗∗ gave the batsman out.
I like watching tennis more than any other ∗∗∗
When the ∗∗∗ reached 500 runs, the team declared.
We watched the game from the ∗∗∗
I listened to the ∗∗∗ on the radio.

Spelling

Each of the following words ends in *ner*.
Use the clues to help you to fill in the missing letters.

* * * n e r	*a person who races*
* * * n e r	*the first in a race*
* * * n e r	*a meal*
* * * n e r	*a flag*
* * * n e r	*the way of doing a thing*
* * * * n e r	*eat less to become this*
* * * * n e r	*a tool for turning nuts*
* * * * * n e r	*one who starts*

Alphabetical Order

It is important to be able to use a dictionary whenever you need to check the spelling or meaning of a word. The words in a dictionary are arranged in *alphabetical order*. Words that have the same first letter are arranged in the alphabetical order of their second letters.

If the first two letters are the same, the words are arranged according to their third letters, and so on.

The words in these groups are arranged in alphabetical order:

hand   help   high   hour   hunt
bolt   bomb   bone   book   boom
chain   chalk   chant   charm   chart

Arrange these letters in alphabetical order:

g   m   b   f   n   k   p   z   h

Now put the words in each of the following groups into alphabetical order:

football   rounders   cricket   swimming   netball
ball   back   bat   bail   base
run   right   rest   round   race

Write some names for each of the following, putting them in alphabetical order:

indoor games   towns   surnames of your friends

Writing

Write about an exciting game that you have played.

Pretend that you are a radio commentator. Write a script describing a game or match as it is actually taking place, and, if you can, record your script on a tape-recorder.

Further Work

Choose a sport, such as tennis, football or cricket, and find out about its history. Then write a short account of how the sport began, and how it developed into the sport we know today.

Draw or paint a picture of a player in action. The picture could show a goalkeeper making a good save, a shooter scoring a goal in netball, or, perhaps, a batsman being clean-bowled.

What games do you play in the playground? Describe one of them, and make a list of the rules.

Invent a new game. Draw up a list of rules, and describe how the game is played.

Can you complete the following finger-game and add the rest of the words?

Here is the church
And here the steeple

Describe any other finger-game that you know.

Write down any rhymes and chants that you use for different playground games. Make up a new rhyme of your own about one of your favourite games.

2 Shadows

Then, on tiptoe,
Off go I
To a white-washed
Wall near by,
Where, for secret
Company,
My small shadow
Waits for me.

Still and stark,
Or stirring—so
All I'm doing
He'll do too.
Quieter than
A cat he mocks
My walk, my gestures,
Clothes and looks.

Walter de la Mare

Shadows come and go with light. When the sun shines, shadows are formed by the shapes of objects, people and creatures. When the sun is low, either in the morning or the evening, the shadows grow long, and look quite different from the things and people that have caused them. At night there are many shadows. As you walk between street lamps, your shadow will move in front of you or behind you, changing shape as you come closer to a light or move further away from it. The gleaming headlights of a car, the beam of a bright torch and the flickering flames of a bonfire at night all make different shadows that move and seem to have a life of their own.

Starting Points

Why are shadows usually dark?

At what time of day are shadows at their smallest?

Which things have shadows that are not joined to them?

Describe any strange shadows you have seen.

Have you ever been frightened by a shadow? Describe how it happened.

Describe any game that you play with shadows.

Words to Use

Look at the second verse of the poem again.
What do the following words mean in the poem?

stirring   mocks   gestures

If you are not sure, look them up in a dictionary.

What do the words *shade* and *shady* mean?

What two things that hold back the light have the word *shade* as part of their names?

What does it mean to *shadow* somebody?

Spelling

Notice that the word *shade* changes its final letter, *e*, to *y* to make *shady*. Do the same with each of the following words, and write the pairs of words in your word book.

stone   bone   taste   gentle   ice

Dictionary Work

Here are some words that might be used to describe different shadows. Find out from a dictionary the meanings of any words that you are not sure about.

*strange   eerie   mysterious   ugly   squat
beautiful   flitting   dancing   creeping
spreading   changing   vanishing*

Writing

What do you think caused each of the different shadows on this page? What do some of the shadows remind you of? Write a story about one of them.

Write a story about someone who lost his shadow, or who found he had someone else's shadow.

Write a poem called 'My Shadow'.

Further Work

When the sun is shining, see what strange or interesting shadows you can find. Make drawings of some of the shapes, and describe what they remind you of.

What shadow shapes can you make with your arms, legs and body?

Make a shadowgraph show. Hang a sheet in a doorway, at a window, or across a frame.
Light up the screen with a bright torch.
(The sort that focuses is best.) Hold up your hands between the torch and the screen, and use your fingers to make shadow faces of people and creatures on the screen. Cut out pieces of card to make hats, beards, pipes, ears, beaks and other shapes that you cannot form with your fingers. Think of some simple plays for your shadow people to act.

A *silhouette* is a shadow outline of the side view of a person's face (his or her *profile*). Make some silhouettes of your friends. Look at each person's profile against a window, or use a torch or a lamp to make a shadowgraph of the profile on a hanging piece of cloth. Cut the silhouette out of black paper, and stick it on a white background.

9

3 Beside the Sea

High up among the girders of the pier,
Under the dark planking of the pier,
They perch and sing:
A boy with tarry legs, and lower,
A girl in blue jeans.
Suddenly he leans—
Heedless of us beneath him,
Heedless of twisted ankle and broken bones—
And with a whoop comes clattering down
Among the stones.

John Walsh

10

Starting Points

Do you like the seaside? If you do, what appeals to you most about it? Is it swimming, paddling, making sand-castles, fishing from the pier, or watching Punch and Judy?

Describe other things that you like about the seaside. Do you prefer a sandy beach or one with pebbles? What do you like to do in places where there are rocks, caves or cliffs?

Have you ever jumped from rocks, a sea-wall or a pier, like the boy in the poem? Describe what happened.

Have you ever walked or played underneath a pier? Describe what it was like, and what you noticed there.

How do you think the boy got *tarry* legs?

Describe a seaside place you have been to, or one you would particularly like to visit.

Words to Use

Use five of these words in sentences about things to see or do at the seaside:

*waves   clattering   pebbles   seaweed
fishing-tackle   breakwater   harbour   sailing
rowing   cruising   diving   floating   drifting*

Using Capital Letters

Capital letters are used for the first letters of:

1   the first word in a sentence

2   the names of people:
Mary Elliott   *John Wood*   *Mr B. Smith*
Mrs D. Brown

3   the names of days and months:
Sunday   *Wednesday*   *January*   *December*

4   the names of streets, places and towns:
High Road   *Hawthorne Close*   *East Brent*
Manchester

5   the important words in the titles of books and poems:
Alice in Wonderland   *'At the Seaside'*

6   the first word in each line of a poem:
When I was down beside the sea
A wooden spade they gave to me
To dig the sandy shore.

Rewrite the following sentences, using capital letters where you think they are needed:

i have just finished the story of black beauty.
on saturday i went to brighton for the day with michael and janet.
mr and mrs hayes have invited us to stay with them in august.

Make up and write six sentences that need capital letters according to the six rules you have been given.

Spelling Game

Use your dictionary to find out which word in each of the following groups is spelled wrongly. Write out each of the incorrect words, with the correct spelling beside it.

crab   mussel   oister   lobster
pier   promenade   bandstand   peble
rowing   sailing   steeming   surfing
sea-gull   sharke   seal   herring
water   waves   fome   spray

Now make up some lists of your own, and see if your partner can find the mistakes.

Writing

Imagine that you have met an old sailor at the seaside. Write down a conversation you have with him, in which he describes some of the wonderful experiences he has had.

You are sitting alone on a sunny beach, when you hear a cry for help. Write the story of what happens next.

Write a poem about all the ways in which you enjoy the seaside.

Further Work

Make a seaside frieze. First, paint a background of waves and sky. Then, paint and cut out shells, pebbles, fish, crabs, boats and a pier to paste on the background.

Spike Milligan once wrote:

Strapped on thirteen life-jackets, grasped my surf-board and hurled myself into the kiddies' paddling pool.

Draw the picture that these words make you think of.

Make a display of seashells. Find out their names and label them clearly.

Make a model of a rowing-boat or yacht out of stiff paper or card. Paint your boat, and give it a name.

With a partner, make up a television interview with a mermaid or merman. If you can, use a tape-recorder to record the interview.

Make up a group mime about the seaside, with each person miming a different activity, such as wading into cold waves, paddling on a stony beach, splashing through shallow water, climbing on rocks, surfing, or water-skiing.

Collect post-cards from different seaside places. Display them around a large map, and connect each card with the place it came from by using thick thread.

4 Trees

The Oak is called the King of Trees,
The Aspen quivers in the breeze,
The Poplar grows up straight and tall,
The Pear tree spreads along the wall,
The Sycamore gives pleasant shade,
The Willow droops in watery glade,
The Fir Tree useful timber gives.

Sara Coleridge

Starting Points

Can you find each of the trees in the poem in the pictures on this page?

Why do you think the oak is called the *King of Trees* in the poem?

Where do willow trees usually grow? Why are they often called *weeping willows*?

What sort of seeds has the sycamore? What games are played with them?

Do you ever play conkers? What are the rules of the game?

Trees look different at different times of the year. Describe what changes you have noticed taking place in the appearance of trees during the different seasons of the year.

Describe a time when you climbed a tree, and tell about any difficulties you had.

Words to Use

These words could be used to describe the size and appearance of a tree:

*tall   lofty   slender   graceful   gnarled
spreading   swaying   massive   smooth*

Here is a sentence using two of the words:

*The branches of the tall tree looked graceful
against the sky.*

These words could be used to describe the movement of leaves:

falling   fluttering   drifting   floating   quivering

Here is a sentence using two of the words:

*The leaves were fluttering and drifting down
from the trees.*

Use some of the words from each group to write a short description of any trees that you have seen.

Describing Where Things Are

Each of the following groups of words, called *phrases*, describes where things are:

*in the wood   at the fence
on the branch   up the tree
by the river   to the field*

Use each of the phrases in a sentence.
For example:

I saw many strange birds in the wood.

14

Tree Puzzles

Copy these puzzles on squared paper and fill in the missing words.

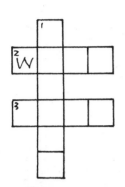

ACROSS
2 a tree supplies this
3 grows on a twig in spring

DOWN
1 a large group of trees

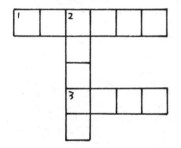

ACROSS
1 an 'arm' of a tree
3 takes in water

DOWN
2 seed of the oak

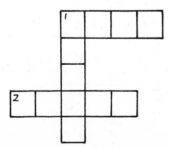

ACROSS
1 grows from a branch
2 a main branch

DOWN
1 the stem of a tree

Writing

Write a story about someone who climbed a tree and was not able to get down again.

Write a poem called 'Autumn in the Forest'.

Write about a tree blown down in a gale.

Further Work

In a group, paint the trunk and branches of a large tree. Use coloured tissue-paper to make leaves, flowers and seeds to paste on the branches.

Make a collection of leaves from different trees. Press the leaves between sheets of damp newspaper, with books laid on top to keep them flat. When the leaves are dry, mount them on a large sheet of paper, and label each one.

In the autumn, collect different tree seeds. Plant one of each type in a separate pot of moist bulb-fibre. Keep the fibre damp and grow some young trees of your own.

Make some leaf prints, using temperapaste or printing ink, and put them on display. Take some bark rubbings of different tree trunks, using thin paper and a wax crayon, and put these on display.

5 Ruins and Relics

There's no smoke in the chimney,
And the rain beats on the floor:
There's no glass in the window,
There's no wood in the door;
The heather grows behind the house,
And the sand lies before.

Mary Coleridge

Starting Points

Look at the picture of the ruined house.

What sort of people probably lived in it?
What kind of work did they do? Why did the
house become ruined?

Have you ever visited a ruined castle or
cathedral? What do you like about such places?

Are there any ruined buildings near your home?

Why is it dangerous to play in a ruined building?

What are *relics*? Describe any that you have
seen in a museum.

What kinds of things can we learn about
people from their relics?

Words to Use

How many words can you find to describe the picture of the house and your feelings about it? Here are some to start your list:

old   ruined   decayed   empty   deserted   lonely

Use some of the words you have collected to write sentences about the house in the picture, about an old castle, and about a ruined windmill. For example:

The old, ruined house stood in a deserted garden.

Now look at the pictures of relics on this page. Write a sentence to describe each one. The following words may help you:

fossil   ancient   bygone   antique   remains preserved   delicate   crumbling   faded discoloured

Spelling

Copy these puzzles on squared paper, and use the clues to solve them:

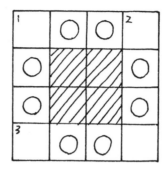

ACROSS
1   *not warm*
3   *sound of car horn*

DOWN
1   *water bird*
2   *stolen goods*

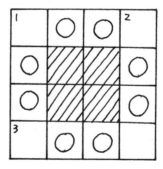

ACROSS
1   *a ring of metal or plastic*
3   *used by a carpenter*

DOWN
1   *cry of an owl*
2   *used for paddling or fishing*

Make up a puzzle of your own with *oo* words. You could use these:

roof   tool   fool   root

17

Shortened Words

In the poem, *there's* is used to show that two words, *there* and *is*, have been shortened into one word. A raised comma, called an *apostrophe*, is put in to show that the letter *i* has been left out. Here are some more shortened words:

here's   where's   we're   you're   I'll   she'll he'll   can't   haven't   hasn't   it's   what's I'd   I'm

We use shortened words like these a great deal when we are talking. Explain what each of them means in full, and try to find some others.

Choose three shortened words to use in a message for a friend, and write down your message.

Writing

Imagine that you and a friend discover an old, ruined building. You peer in through a door or window. Write a story or poem about what you find.

Further Work

Find out about a ruined building or a disused railway line or canal in your district, or in a place you have visited. Write a description of what is there now, and what you imagine it was like when it was new.

Choose a building you know well. Imagine a hundred years have passed and the building is now in ruins. Paint a picture of what it looks like.

Imagine that you have dug up some relics in your garden. Write a newspaper report about the importance of your finds.

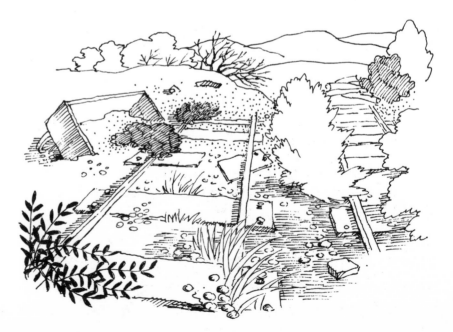

6 Dragons

There have been so many legends and stories about dragons that it is easy to understand why people once believed that they really did exist. A dragon was thought by most people to be a fierce, evil creature, which roared thunderously and breathed out fire and smoke. Dragons were said to live in dark caverns, beneath deep lakes, or up in the clouds. But there were some people who did not believe that dragons were evil. In ancient China, the dragon was worshipped as a god who made the wind blow and the rain fall.

When the Romans occupied Britain, their standards were decorated with a dragon, and this symbol eventually became the badge of Wales. The ships that carried the fierce Vikings to invade Britain had dragon-heads carved on their prows. The coat of arms of the City of London is held up by a pair of dragons. The shield bears the red cross of Saint George, the patron saint of England, who is supposed to have fought and killed a ferocious dragon.

Starting Points

Why did people in the past believe in dragons?

What animals that still live today may have caused people to think that they had seen dragons?

What tiny creatures would appear as fierce and dangerous as dragons if they were much larger?

What reasons might people long ago have had for believing that storms were caused by dragons?

Which modern machines might be thought of as dragons?

Describe the fiercest dragon you have read about.

Words to Use

Find the following words in the passage about dragons:

legend exist evil caverns worshipped occupied symbol invade prows ferocious

Look up the words in a dictionary, and write a sentence about each one to show that you know its meaning.

Explain what each of these is:

a flag   a badge   a shield   a Roman standard a coat of arms

Nouns and Adjectives

The names of people, creatures and things are called *nouns*. Words that describe people, creatures and things are called *adjectives*. Adjectives describe nouns. For example:

The fierce *dragon lived in a* dark *cave.*

Find four other adjectives in the passage about dragons.

Play an adjective game in groups of four. Each person will need ten pieces of card, each about 4 × 2 cm. On five of the cards, he or she should write different *nouns*, such as *dog*, *elephant*, or *tree*, and on the other five, different *adjectives*, such as *friendly*, *large*, or *tall*. All the group's cards should then be mixed together, and put in a pile, face down. Each player then takes a card in turn, places it face up and decides whether it is a noun or an adjective. On the next turn, each player takes a second card and decides if it will make a suitable adjective and noun pair with the first card, such as *friendly dog*, or *tall tree*. If it does, then the player keeps the pair together, but if not, he returns one card to the bottom of the pile, face down. The first person to make five pairs is the winner.

Write a story to follow this newspaper headline:

POTHOLER DISCOVERS DRAGON'S CAVE

Spelling

How many complete words ending in *ck* can you find across and down this stairway? Notice that some lines have more than one word, such as *crack* and *rack*, *click* and *lick*. Make a list of the words you find.

Writing

Imagine that you were alive at a time when people believed in dragons. One day, you were caught in a violent storm. Write a story about the dragon in the sky.

Further Work

Find out about *heraldry*. Discover why designs were painted on shields and badges, and why coats of arms came into use. Then design and paint a large shield for a knight who fought dragons.

Paint a picture of a fierce dragon guarding its treasure in a cave, or a sky dragon which brings wind, clouds and rain.

Make a collage picture of St George fighting the dragon. Use silver foil or milk-bottle tops and egg cartons for the dragon's scaly body.

Read the story about St George and the dragon. Make a dragon's head out of papier-mâché, a shield and sword out of thick card, and act the play in your group.

Read *The Reluctant Dragon* by Kenneth Grahame (Collins), and *Dragon Slayer* by Rosemary Sutcliff (Puffin).

7　Daybreak

You are asleep in bed. Gradually you begin to wake up. You feel the warmth of the bedclothes around you, and the softness of the pillow beneath your head. Drowsily you hear sounds outside that tell you it is morning: a pattering of feet, the twittering of birds, leaves rustling, the roaring of traffic, dogs barking and bells chiming. You turn, stretch a little and open your eyes. There is daylight coming through the curtains. You hear the sound of gurgling water, the rattle of crockery, and voices chattering downstairs. Is it time to get up already? What day is it? Suddenly you remember, and you jump out of bed, go over to the window and look out. It is morning and the day has begun.

Starting Points

How do you like to wake up—slowly or suddenly?

Describe how you woke up this morning.

How do you feel and what do you think about when you first awaken?

What are the first sounds that you hear in the morning?

How can you tell when you wake up whether it is a weekday, or a Saturday or Sunday?

How can you tell what time of the year it is and what the weather is like when you wake up?

What does your room look like in the early morning light?

What are you likely to see from your bedroom window in the early morning?

Describe a time when you woke up in a place quite different from your own home.

Words to Use

Warmth and *softness* are two words that describe things we feel when we are lying in bed. What other words can you think of?

Explain what *gradually* and *drowsily* mean.

What other words mean the same or nearly the same as *beneath*?

In how many different ways can you use the word *stretch*?

Make a list of words that describe noises you hear as you wake up in the morning. Write them in your word book.

Using Sound Words

Some words in the passage about waking up tell us a great deal about sounds. For example:

pattering twittering rustling roaring
barking chiming

Find three other words in the passage that describe noises.

Make a list of sounds you often hear. Find a word to describe each sound. Choose six sounds and write a sentence about each one.

Words that Tell How Things are Done

Look at these three sentences:

I awoke suddenly.
I slowly clambered out of bed.
Gradually the light grew stronger.

Suddenly, slowly and *gradually* are words that tell how a thing is done. They are called *adverbs,* because each one describes a verb. Many adverbs end in *ly*. For example:

quickly softly bravely proudly brightly

Use each of these adverbs in a sentence of your own.

Play an adverb game. Each person in the group should choose an action to mime, such as *dig, sew, listen, creep,* or *climb.* Then everyone takes it in turns to mime his or her action in a certain way. For example, *dig wearily, sew carefully* or *climb painfully.* The first person to guess the adverb being mimed wins a point.

Writing

Imagine that you are sleeping in a place where you would especially like to be, such as in a tent, in a country cottage or on board a ship. Write about what it is like to wake up in your new surroundings.

Write a poem called 'Morning Sounds'.

Spelling

Pattering, twittering and *rattling* are all spelt with a double *t*. So are the words in the puzzle below. Use the clues to help you to fill in the missing letters.

b*tt**   *container made of glass*
*ett**   *sent by post*
**ttl*   *a fight between armies*
**tt*e   *cows and oxen*
k*tt**   *water is boiled in it*
*utt**   *channel at roadside or below roof*
**tte*   *waste paper*
**tt*r   *to speak in a low voice*

Further Work

Make a chart to show the different times at which the sun rises in each month of the year.

Paint a picture of the sun rising. The sunrise could be over a town or city, with an outline of buildings, chimneys and spires against the glowing sky, or it could be over a forest, mountains, or the sea.

Write out the words of the hymn 'Morning has Broken', and decorate the page with patterns and pictures.

8 Let's Send a Letter

This is the night mail crossing the border,
Bringing the cheque and the postal order,
Letters for the rich, letters for the poor,
The shop at the corner and the girl next door . . .

Letters of thanks, letters from banks,
Letters of joy from girl and boy,
Receipted bills and invitations
To inspect new stock or visit relations . . .

Letters with holiday snaps to enlarge in,
Letters with faces scrawled in the margin,
Letters from uncles, cousins and aunts,
Letters to Scotland from the South of France . . .

W. H. Auden

Starting Points

Do you sometimes get letters? Who sends them?
What are they about?

What kinds of letters do you enjoy most?

What kinds of letters do you not have to
answer?

When would it be better to write a letter than
to telephone?

Why are stamps on letters, parcels and
post-cards cancelled by the Post Office?

Would you like to be a postman?
Give your reasons.

How much does it cost to send a letter?

How could you send money through the post?

Words to Use
What do these words mean?

telegram   postage   delivery   air mail   sorter receipted bill   postal order   cheque
Use each word or phrase in a sentence.

Pronouns
Nouns are the names of people, places and things. In a sentence or passage which mentions the same person, place or thing several times, we normally replace the noun with another word after the first time it is used. For example:

The postman sometimes brings me a letter.
He puts it through the letter-box.

In the second sentence, *he* has been used instead of *postman,* and *it* has been used instead of *letter. He* and *it* are called *pronouns.* A pronoun takes the place of a noun. Here are some other pronouns:

she   him   her   them   I   me   us   his hers   ours

How many can you add to the list?

Play a pronoun game. Each member of the group takes it in turns to give a sentence with at least two unnecessary nouns. The next person changes the unnecessary nouns into pronouns. Score a point for each correct pronoun. For example:

George gave the pen to Margaret, and Margaret used the pen.
George gave the pen to Margaret, and she *used* it.   (2 points)

Mark will go and buy some bread, if Mark and Jane need bread.
Mark will go and buy some bread, if they *need* it.   (2 points)

Writing
There are a number of rules to follow when you are writing a letter.

1   Your address should be written in the top right-hand corner, followed by the date.

2   Dear . . . , is written on the left-hand side, on a separate line at the beginning.

3   Yours sincerely, is written on a separate line at the end, followed by your signature. (*Yours faithfully,* is used at the end of a letter which begins with *Dear Sir.*)

Sort out the following letter. Write it out in its proper form, putting in full stops and capital letters where they are needed.

23 Lodge Road, Eastbourne, Sussex, BN27 1OT
20th June 1977
Dear Sir, I am sorry I kept Ian from school yesterday, but he had a cold. I kept him in bed he is better now I hope you will excuse his absence. Yours faithfully, Eva Brooks

Draw an envelope, and write the name and address of your school on it.

Spelling
When we add *full* to a word, the final *l* is dropped. For example:

cheerful   handful   spoonful

How many other words ending in *ful* can you find? Write them in your word book.

Further Work
Make up a scene to act about a postman on his round. Perhaps he is worried by a dog, or it is raining heavily. Think of other things that might happen to him.

Collect different postage stamps from old envelopes, and stick them on a display sheet in order of price. Make a separate display of cards and envelopes with clear postmarks.

Design a postage-stamp to celebrate a special day or event in your town. Paint a large design to put on the wall.

Write a letter to someone in your class who is ill at home or in hospital, or to someone else you know who is ill.

Write the letter you would most like to receive tomorrow morning.

27

9 Wishes

I wish I was—
A new king walking proudly towards my throne
Slowly . . .
Kneeling to receive my crown
Proudly . . .

Niall Macaulay

'I wish' is an expression we all use from time to time. Sometimes we wish for the impossible, like the boy in the poem. Sometimes we simply wish to be allowed to stay up late. Think about your own wishes.

Starting Points

What is your chief wish? Is it a piece of day-dreaming, like that in the poem, or is it something that could happen?

What do you wish to become when you grow up?

Have you ever pulled a wishbone with someone? Did you make a wish? Do you believe that such wishes can come true?

Have you ever made a wish over a wishing-well, for example, and found that it did come true?

Have you ever made wishes about other people? What were they?

Words to Use

Look at these words. They all describe ways in which people dream about or wish for things.

proudly   hopefully   longingly

The following words are also sometimes used about dreams or wishes:

desire   sigh for   daydream   imagine   love

Choose five of these words, and use each of them in sentences about something you would like to have or do.

Using Commas

The comma is used to make a slight pause in a sentence, for example, when a list of things is given:

Johnny collects conkers, sycamore seeds, acorns and shells.

Notice that a comma is used after each item except the one which is followed by *and*.

Write these sentences, putting in the missing commas:

When I went shopping I bought a comic an ice cream and some stamps.
In my garden there are roses lupins pansies and dahlias.
The shop-window was a jumble of toys foreign coins old magazines and picture post-cards.

Write a sentence in which you mention some of the things in your pocket or bag.

Spelling

There is a rule in English spelling that *i* comes before *e* except after *c*. Here are some examples:

chief   siege   shield   receive   ceiling

Can you think of any more? Make a list.

There are exceptions to the rule. For example:

their   neither

Can you think of any more?

Writing

You have been granted three wishes. What do you wish for? Write about each wish, explaining your reasons for making it.

Imagine that you wish never to grow up. Write the story of what happens as your wish comes true, and you watch your friends and relations growing older while you remain the same age as you are now.

Further Work

Draw or paint pictures of wishes that you would like to come true for people you know. They could be happy, funny, strange, or even frightening.

Make up a play about a greedy man and his wife who are granted three wishes. Act it with your friends.

Make a collage picture of all the different things that are supposed to make wishes come true, such as wishing-wells, fountains, wishbones and lucky numbers.

Make a list of things to do at special times to make wishes come true, for example, turning over the money in your pocket when you see a new moon, making a cross on your shoe when you see a black cat, and stirring a Christmas pudding.

Write a poem which begins with the words: *I wish*.

10 Kites

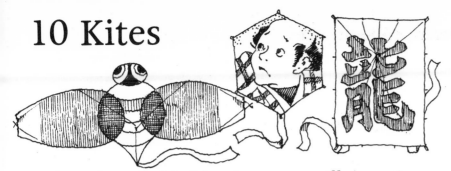

When the wind is blowing, you will sometimes see kites flying over parks, commons or hills, or beside the sea. There are three main types of kites: flat kites, bow kites and box kites. Flat kites are the most popular. They are made in many different shapes, but each one has a tail to balance it.

In China, kite-flying is a popular pastime for adults as well as children. People fly kites in the shapes of birds, butterflies, dragons and fish. Some are fitted with reeds that give out wailing noises in the wind. Reeds were first used long ago to frighten evil spirits away from the kites.

The Japanese have an exciting sport of kite-fighting. They coat the upper part of a kite's string with powdered glass, which forms a hard edge. Each flyer sails his kite up to that of his opponent, and tries to cut the string of the other kite by giving his own string a sharp downward jerk.

Kites have also been flown for useful purposes. In the eighteenth century, Benjamin Franklin proved that lightning is electricity by attracting a charge from a thunder cloud down the cord of a kite. Kites have been used to carry instruments for weather forecasting, and to take electric cables across rivers. During the Second World War, kites were used as distress signals by airmen who had been forced down into the sea. The survivors of an air crash climbed into a rubber dinghy and flew a large yellow kite which helped rescue planes to spot them.

Starting Points

Describe the best way to make a kite fly.

Where are the best places for flying kites? Where could kite-flying be dangerous?

Tell about a time when you saw a kite getting into difficulties.

Describe the different kinds of kites that you have seen flying or have flown yourself. Which type do you think is the best?

Describe any other occasions you have heard or read about when kites have been flown for useful purposes. Can you think of other times when kites might prove useful?

Words to Use

Sort the following words into two groups: those that are to do with going up, and those that are to do with going down.

dived   dipped   rose   fell   sank   dropped
soared   plunged   swooped   ascended   descended

Now make up a sentence using any of the words to describe the movement of each of the following:

a kite   a plane   a hawk
an arrow   a lift   a rocket

Writing

Write a story about a kite that escaped from its owner and flew away to another country.

Imagine that you live in Japan, and are going to take part in a kite fight. Write the story of the fight, describing how you bring down your opponent's kite, which is made in the shape of a fierce hawk.

Write a poem about a kite which begins:
High in the sky.

Building Sentences

Look at these words: *kite   flies   sky*

Here is a sentence using the words:

The kite flies in the sky.

Here is another, more descriptive sentence, using the same three words:

The large, yellow kite flies above in the blue sky.

Build an interesting sentence from each of the following groups of words, using the three words in each group in any order.

birds   fly   trees   *fire   smoke   grass*
cat   creeps   bushes   *rain   lights   reflections*
horse   galloped   street

Spelling

Use the clues to help you to fill in the missing letters.

k n * *	*tied with string*
k n * *	*to make wool into clothing*
k n * *	*leg joint*
k n * *	*to understand*
k n * *	*door handle*
k n * * *	*to hit*
k n * * *	*needs to be sharp*
k n * * * * *	*finger joint*

Further Work

Make a kite of your own. You will need two thin garden sticks or canes, a reel of thin string, a sheet of paper, tissue-paper or polythene, and a curtain-ring.

Glue and bind the two sticks together, as shown in the first diagram. Cut notches across the ends of the sticks. Slot the string into the notches, and tie it tightly to form the frame of the kite. Cut the covering of the kite around the frame, leaving a margin, as shown by the dotted line in the second diagram. Then bend the edges of the covering over the edges of the frame and glue them down.

Fix a piece of string 75 cm long to the top of the kite, loop it through the curtain ring several times and fix it to the bottom of the kite. Fix another piece of string 55 cm long across the kite in the same way. Make a tail of string about five times the length of the kite and fix it to the bottom of the kite. Lastly, tie the end of the reel of string securely to the curtain-ring. When you fly the kite, pull the curtain-ring up or down or from side to side until the kite flies steadily.

Draw a picture of the following limerick:

A foolish young fellow named White
Was flying a very big kite,
But the wind was too strong
And he held on too long,
And soon he was blown out of sight.

Paint a frieze of clouds and sky on a windy day. Cut out kites of different types, with flowing tails. Decorate them with faces or bright patterns. Paste them on the background of the sky. Copy out a poem you have written or read about kites and add it to the frieze.

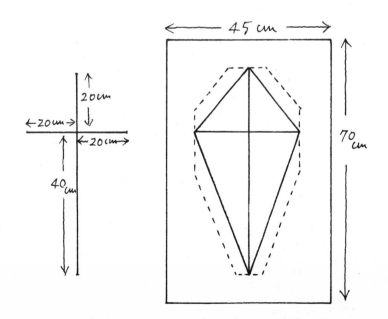

33

11 Feeling Hungry?

When the girl returned, some hours later, she carried a tray with a cup of fragrant tea steaming on it; and a plate piled up with very hot buttered toast, cut thick, very brown on both sides, with the butter running through the holes in great golden drops, like honey from the honeycomb. The smell of that buttered toast simply talked to Toad, and with no uncertain voice, talked of warm kitchens, of breakfasts on bright frosty mornings, of cosy parlour firesides on winter evenings, when one's ramble was over and slippered feet were propped on the fender; of the purring of contented cats, and the twitter of sleepy canaries. Toad sat up on end once more, dried his eyes, sipped his tea and munched his toast, and soon began talking freely about himself.

Kenneth Grahame

Starting Points

The meal that Toad had was a simple one. What meals do you enjoy most?

What tastes or smells of food remind you of things you have done at other times?

When do you usually feel most hungry? Describe things you do that make you feel hungry.

Which meal of the day do you enjoy most?

What do you especially like about eating out in a café or restaurant, or on a picnic?

What foods have the most attractive smells when they are being cooked?

Which foods do you think are best eaten raw?

What sounds tell you that a meal is being prepared?

What precautions should be taken in preparing and cooking food?

How many different ways do you know of cooking eggs? Which way do you prefer?

Words to Use

The following words refer to smell, taste, eating, drinking and cooking. Look up any of them that you are not sure about in a dictionary.

fragrant   spicy   tasty   delicious   crunchy
crisp   crumbly   sip   chew   munch   swallow
gulp   bake   boil   fry   grill   toast   roast
stew

Choose five of the words, and use them in sentences about food that you have enjoyed.

Kinds of Nouns

Nouns can be divided into three types, according to their sex: *male, female* or *neuter*. For example, *man* is a male noun, *woman* is a female noun, and *pencil* is a neuter noun.

Play a game with nouns. Give your partner several male and female nouns. He or she must give the opposite of each one. For example:

girl (boy)   bull (cow)

Here are some male nouns to start you off:

brother   king   prince   lion

Perhaps you could give a neuter noun sometimes, just for fun.

Spelling

Use the clues to help you find the names of the following shops:

g * * * * g * * * * * s   *where apples are bought*
b * * * r *   *where bread is bought*
* u t * * * * *   *where meat is bought*
* * s h m * * g e * *   *where fish is bought*
g * * c e * *   *where sugar and butter are bought*

35

Writing

Invent a simple recipe for making custard, scrambled eggs, or a cake.

Prepare a menu for a school dinner that you would particularly enjoy.

Invent a fun recipe. How would you make Hippopotamus Hotpot, Elephant Pudding, or Tortoise Tart?

Further Work

Paint a picture of the inside of your favourite food shop, or design an advertising poster for your favourite food or drink.

Make a display of food packages and labels. Beneath each one, write a short account of how the food was produced and where the ingredients came from.

Choose several popular foods and find out how many of your class like each of them. Make a chart to show the results.

Find songs and poems about food and drink, and choose one verse to write out and illustrate. If there is no verse that you particularly like, write one of your own.

Make up a play about a family eating a meal in a restaurant where everything goes wrong. Soup is upset, the food is cold and the bill is too dear.

12 Finding Your Way

A famous story about a maze comes from the Island of Crete, where, long ago, King Minos had a maze, called a *labyrinth*, built beneath his palace. In the centre of the labyrinth lived the *Minotaur*—a monster with the head of a bull and the body of a man. Each year, King Minos sent soldiers to Athens and demanded that they should bring back seven young men and women to be fed to the Minotaur as an offering.

One year, a prince named Theseus travelled with the prisoners, determined to kill the Minotaur. When the young people arrived in Crete, the king imprisoned them in a dungeon, planning to send them into the labyrinth on the following morning.

That night, Ariadne, the king's daughter, stole secretly to the dungeon, and let Theseus out. She gave him a sword and a ball of silk thread to help him to find his way out of the maze.

Theseus crept through the labyrinth, unwinding the thread as he followed the twisting, zigzag passages towards the centre. At last, he turned a corner and saw the monster waiting for him. As it rushed at him, Theseus seized its horns and thrust his sword into its neck. The Minotaur sank to the ground, dying.

Theseus followed the thread back to the entrance, where he found Ariadne waiting. Together, they released the young people from the dungeon and hurried to the harbour, where they all boarded a boat and set sail for Athens.

Starting Points

Have you ever been in a maze? Describe what it was like, and how you felt while you were trying to find your way out.

Why is it much more difficult to find your way out of a real maze than to trace your way round a diagram of a maze?

Can you think of any other method by which Theseus could have found his way back to the entrance of the labyrinth?

Describe any game that you have played in which you left signs for others to follow.

Words to Use

Use a dictionary to find the meaning of each of the following words:

labyrinth demanded determined zigzag seized thrust offering released

Explain what each word means.

Make a collection of words to do with finding or losing your way. Here are some examples:

lost found search recognised puzzled confused bewildered

Find the Treasure

Play this game with a partner. Take it in turns to direct the other person, an explorer, to the treasure in the centre of the maze. The explorer must follow his instructions exactly, so the directions must be correct. Use such words as:

turn left turn right go forward go backwards return advance stop about turn

You lose a point each time you direct the explorer into a dead-end passage. If you direct the explorer into the monster's lair, he or she is devoured instantly, and you lose five points. Score ten points when the explorer reaches the treasure, and another ten when he has carried it safely out of the maze.

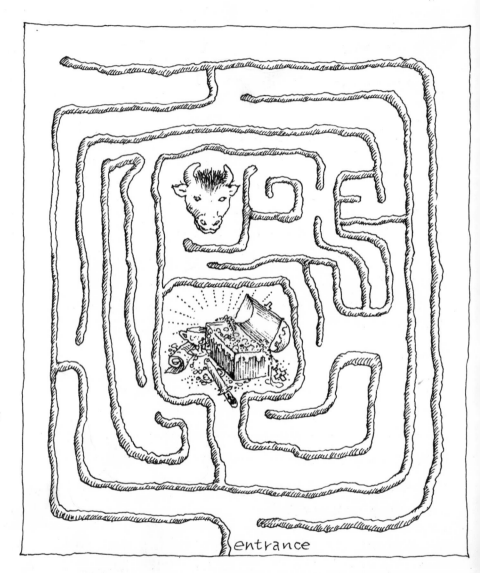

entrance

Using Verbs

Every sentence should have a *verb*. Many verbs tell us what somebody or something is doing. For example:

Theseus crept *through the labyrinth.*
The Minotaur sank *to the ground.*

Look through the story of Theseus, and collect the verbs that describe the different movements he made in the labyrinth. Choose five of the verbs and use each one in a separate sentence of your own.

Play a game of miming verbs. Each person in the group takes it in turn to mime one of the following verbs:

creep   limp   dig   climb   sweep   wave
cut   read   paint   drink

The first person to guess each mime scores a point. When you have used all the verbs, think of others of your own. To make sure that a word is a verb, check that you can use *I* in front of it.

Further Work

Design your own maze. Do not make it too complicated. See whether your partner can direct you through your maze without making mistakes.

Write a story about the maze you have designed. Describe how someone gets lost in it while he or she is looking for treasure. What happens?

Paint a picture of Theseus fighting the Minotaur.

Design a maze pattern that could be used to decorate a bowl, a dress, or, perhaps, a wall.

Make a bull's-head mask, using stiff card for the horns, and act the story of Theseus and the Minotaur.

13 The Sun

Because the sun is necessary for life on earth, it was once worshipped as a god, and there are many legends to explain why it appeared to move across the sky each day. The early Egyptians called the sun-god *Ra*, and they believed that he was rowed across the sky in a boat. The Greeks named the sun *Helios*, and told how he drove a golden chariot across the sky, pulled by four white-winged horses.

High in the Andes Mountains, the Aztec Indians of ancient Mexico built a gigantic temple of the sun, and lined its walls with gold.

Every year a handsome young man was chosen to live in the temple as a sun-god, but at the end of the year he was killed as a sacrifice to the sun, so that it would continue to give life back to earth.

Today we know that the sun is not a god, but we realise that without it nothing could live on earth.

Starting Points

What would happen to the earth if the sun stopped shining?

Why is it dangerous to look directly at the sun?

What precautions should you take when sunbathing?

What effect does the sun have on your feelings? How do you feel when you awake on a sunny morning, or when the sun shines after rain or a storm, or during a long walk on a hot day?

Describe what the sun looks like at dawn, at sunset, and on a foggy day in winter.

What is a sundial? How does it work?

When is the sun at its highest in the sky?

Name some flowers that look like the sun.

Words to Use

Put the following words into pairs that have similar meanings:

*sunrise   sunset   sundown   noon   dawn
midday*

Choose one word from each pair and use it in a sentence.

Put these words into order of temperature, starting with the coldest:

hot   sweltering   cool   warm   mild   stifling

Many words have been added to the word *sun* to make new, *compound* words, such as *sunlight* and *sunburn*. Make a collection of compound *sun* words in your word book.

Past and Present

Look at these two sentences:

*Mary talks to her friend.
Mary talked to her friend.*

The first sentence tells us what is happening *now*. The verb *talk* is being used in the *present tense (talks)*. The second sentence tells us what happened in the *past*. The verb is in the *past tense (talked)*.

Many verbs take *ed* when they are used in the past tense. For example:

*walk, walked   jump, jumped   march, marched
wish, wished*

Some verbs double the last letter before adding *ed*. For example:

stop, stopped   drip, dripped   rob, robbed

Some verbs are changed in other ways. For example:

John runs *home.*
John ran *home.*

I see *the postman coming.*
I saw *the postman coming.*

We go *to school today.*
We went *to school today.*

The birds fly *up into the trees.*
The birds flew *up into the trees.*

Write sentences in the past tense, using each of the following verbs in turn:

*run   sing   hide   buy   tell   forget   swim
leave   speak   fight*

Spelling
Use the clues to help you to fill in the missing letters:

* i g h t	*opposite of dark*
* i g h t	*after dark*
* i g h t	*correct*
* i g h t	*sense of seeing*
* * i g h t	*shining*
* * i g h t	*rode in tournaments*
* * i g h t	*measurement from bottom to top*
* * i g h t	*the act of flying*

Writing
Write a poem called 'The Summer Sun'.

Imagine you were alive long ago, before people understood why the sun appears to move across the sky. Write a story of your own to explain the sight.

Further Work
Find out facts about the sun. For example, what it is made of, how far away it is from the earth, how many hours of daylight there are on the shortest and longest days of the year, where the *Land of the Midnight Sun* and the *Land of the Rising Sun* are, and why they are called by these names. Collect together all the information you discover in a book about the sun.

Make a sun frieze. Show the sun in different positions in the sky at different times between dawn and dusk.

Make a collage picture of the sun, using gold and silver foil.

Paint a picture of Helios driving across the sky in his chariot.

14 What's in a Name?

Boys' and Girls' Names

What splendid names for boys there are!
There's Carol like a rolling car—
And Martin like a flying bird—
And Adam like the Lord's First Word—
And Raymond like the Harvest Moon—
And Peter like a piper's tune—
And Alan, like the flowing on
Of water.
And there's John, like John.

What lovely names for girls there are!
There's Stella like the Evening Star—
And Sylvia like a rustling tree—
And Lola like a melody—
And Flora like the flowery morn—
And Sheila like a field of corn—
And Melusina, like the moan
Of water.
And there's Joan, like Joan.

Eleanor Farjeon

Starting Points

Do you think that people's names are important?

Do you like your own name? If not, what would you like to be called?

Are there any names in the poem that you particularly like?

Should children be allowed to choose their own names?

Sometimes we make up names for people. These are called *nicknames*. Do you have a nickname? Do you like it? Do you know the reason for it?

Do nicknames tell us more about people than their own names?

What kinds of towns and villages might these places be, from the sound of their names?

Ugley   Messing   Sandwich   Beer   Maddingley
Barking   Silvertown   Mousehole

Comparing Things with People

Sometimes we speak of things as though they were people. A ship, for instance, is always called *she*. Can you think of other examples?

Look at this sentence. It compares a tree with a person.

The bare arms of the tree stretched out to heaven.

Sentences of this kind help to make a piece of writing more vivid. Make up a similar sentence about each of the following:

a mighty wind
a volcano erupting
a bulldozer
a fast train
waves against a sea-wall

Spelling

Can you give the names of these people? Each of them has the same name as a trade or an occupation.

* a r * * *	*drives a cart*
* a r * * * * *	*works in a garden*
* h e p * * * *	*looks after sheep*
* * u m b * *	*mends water-pipes*
j o * * * *	*joins things together*
* r i * * *	*drives a car or bus*

Writing

Write a story about a person or a place, explaining why the person or place was so named. The name could be comic, curious, creepy, or just unusual. Here are some names to think about:

Mr Pennyfeather   Mr Jingle   Gagool
Samson Brass   Melbury Bubb   Cowbridge
Childerditch   Coton   Poole   Devil's Dyke

Make up a verse or two to add to the following song:

Oranges and lemons,
Say the bells of St Clements.

Two sticks and an apple,
Say the bells of Whitechapel.

Further Work

Draw or paint the kind of animal which might have one of these names:

hippocrump   snapdragonfly   woomerong

Draw pictures of people who are happy, sad, or cruel-looking. Find a suitable name for each of the people, and write the names under the pictures.

Read the story of Rumplestilzkin and act it in your group. You will find the story in a book called *Grimm's Fairy Tales*.

Make a book of names. Write a little about every interesting name that you come across. If you can, explain how the name began. Include pictures of some of the people, places and things in your book.

There were three dwarfs who dwelt on an isle
And the name of the isle was Lone,
And the names of the dwarfs were Alliolyle,
Lallerie and Muzziomone.

What was the isle like? What sort of characters did the dwarfs have? What did they do on the isle? Make up a story or a play about the verse.

15 Score a Bull's-eye

What have you learned? Here are some reminders of the work you have done with this book. Score a bull's-eye for each correct section.

1 Punctuate the following sentences, putting in full stops, commas and capital letters where you think they are needed:

on sunday i went fishing at westwood pond with bill and alan
mrs smith asked me to get her some stamps
a packet of envelopes and a newspaper

2 Arrange the words in the following groups in alphabetical order:

next   gown   field   steal   police   newt   grown steam   fierce

rat   elephant   mouse   antelope   ox   fox bison   ape   reindeer

3 Build sentences using each of the following groups of words:

sailor   island   bottle   tree   roots   gold mountain   cloud   valley

4 Make sentences using each of the following phrases:

in the window   by the sea   at the gate

5 Write what each of the shortened words in these sentences means in full:

How's your brother?
We'll go tomorrow.
I haven't seen him.
This isn't right.

6 From the two lists which follow, find a suitable adjective to go with each noun, and use each pair of words in a sentence.

ADJECTIVE	NOUN
tall	*mouse*
green	*wind*
cold	*tree*
fierce	*door*
timid	*tiger*

7 Write the following sentences in the past tense:

The postman brings the letters every morning.
I hear the sound of thunder.
I see the sun rising in the east.
The cat creeps towards the bird.

8 In the following sentences, use pronouns in place of the nouns in ordinary type.

I told John *that* Mary *would be angry if* John *lost* Mary's *dog.*
The Thames *runs swiftly at this point.*
Susan and Michael *are going on holiday tomorrow.*

9 Decide whether each of the words in ordinary type in the following sentences is a noun, an adjective, a verb, a pronoun or an adverb.

He suddenly ran away.
A huge wave swept *over the* rocks.
We heard *the* great bell *chiming.*

10 Each of the words below follows a spelling rule or pattern that you have learned from this book. Use the clues to help you to find the missing letters.

s * * * l   *has three legs*
f * * l *   *meadow*
c * o * *   *tells the time*
l * * * * e   *small*
s * i * * *   *to fasten with thread*
w * n * * *   *first past the winning-post*
f * * * * t   *a ghost might give you one*
p * * n f * *   *a bruise or cut can be this*

11 Each of the words in this stairword puzzle has something to do with summer. Copy the diagram on squared paper, and use the clues to help you to fill in the words.

ACROSS
1   *cereal plants—wheat, oats, maize*
2   *a gentle bird, like a pigeon*
3   *grows from a branch*
6   *laid in nests*
8   *country road*
10 *used for rowing*

DOWN
2   *sunrise*
3   *home of birds*
4   *sing a s * * * of summer*
5   *summer flower*
7   *for catching the wind*
9   *heard in a cave*

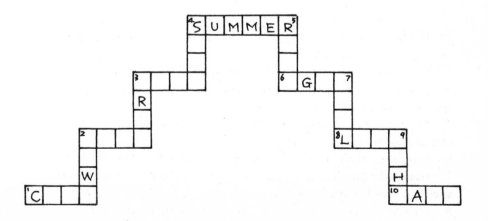

To the Teacher

The sections in each topic have been designed to provide as wide an approach to language development as possible and to link this with interesting and creative activities in other subjects. The general aims of each section are as follows:

Starting Points: to encourage discussion and preliminary writing work on the theme and on specific points arising from it. This work will give pupils the opportunity of first expressing themselves orally and taking part in the interchange of ideas, personal experiences and opinions that will prepare them for the writing suggestions that follow.

Words to Use: to develop understanding of vocabulary used in the introduction or arising from the theme. Used as an adjunct to the work in Talking Points, it provides indirect comprehension practice and, where suitable, introduces short, specific writing exercises.

Writing: offers alternative suggestions for pupils to choose, at the teacher's discretion, an aspect of the topic for the main written work.

Further Work: intended as a miscellany of suggestions from which a choice can be made for pupils to follow individual or group assignments that involve creative activities and integrating other subjects through further reading and research.

Details of specific practice in grammar, sentence construction and spelling to be found under separate headings in each of the topics are as follows:

1   *Games:* spelling: words ending in *ner;* alphabetical order.
2   *Shadows:* spelling: changing words ending in *e* to words ending in *y;* dictionary practice.
3   *Beside the Sea:* using capital letters; spelling: sea words.
4   *Trees:* using phrases with prepositions to build sentences; spelling: words about trees.
5   *Ruins and Relics:* abbreviated words; spelling: words containing *oo.*
6   *Dragons:* nouns and adjectives; spelling: words ending in *ck.*
7   *Daybreak:* building sentences using words about sounds; adverbs; spelling: words containing *tt.*
8   *Let's Send a Letter:* pronouns; spelling: adding *ful* to words.

9   *Wishes:* using commas; spelling: rule for using *ie.*
10   *Kites:* verbs about ascending and descending; building up sentences from word groups; spelling: words beginning with *kn.*
11   *Feeling Hungry?* gender of nouns; spelling: names of food shops.
12   *Finding Your Way:* verbs of movement; spelling: words ending in *tch.*
13   *The Sun:* compound words; present and past tense; spelling: words ending in *ight.*
14   *What's in a Name?* simple metaphors; spelling: names of trades and occupations.
15   *Score a Bull's-eye:* revision exercises and puzzles on the grammar, punctuation, sentence construction and spelling discussed in the book.